Herding South
Poems

Herding South
Poems

Peter Omoko

malthouse
Malthouse Press Limited
Lagos, Benin, Ibadan, Jos, Port-Harcourt, Zaria

© Peter Omoko 2019
First Published 2019
ISBN: 978-978-56575-1-7

Published and manufactured in Nigeria by

Malthouse Press Limited
43 Onitana Street, Off Stadium Hotel Road,
Off Western Avenue, Lagos Mainland
E-mail: malthouselagos@gmail.com
malthouse_press@yahoo.com
Tel: +234 802 600 3203

All rights reserved. No part of this publication may be reproduced, transmitted, transcribed, stored in a retrieval system or translated into any language or computer language, in any form or by any means, electronic, mechanical, magnetic, chemical, thermal, manual or otherwise, without the prior consent in writing of Malthouse Press Limited, Lagos, Nigeria and of the Author.

This book is sold subject to the condition that it shall not by way of trade, or otherwise, be lent, re-sold, hired out, or otherwise circulated without the publisher's prior consent in writing, in any form of binding or cover other than in which it is published and without a similar condition, including this condition, being imposed on the subsequent purchaser.

Distributors:

African Books Collective Ltd
Email: abc@africanbookscollective.com
Website: http://www.africanbookscollective.com

Dedication

To
All those
who lose
their lives
in the senseless
greed of the land

Acknowledgements

I salute profusely the many individuals, groups and institutions whose destinies, actions and inactions ignited the muse that birthed this work: the helpless farmers, pregnant women and innocent children whose necks, labours and homes fell to the sickles, bullets and savagery of blood thirsty herdsmen in different parts of the country; the dispossessed people of the Niger Delta whose crude oil and gas resources enrich the climes of others but leave them wretched; the government who turned blind eye to the plight of the downtrodden; the numerous renegades who assisted in foregrounding poverty in the land and the multitudes who fold their arms as the country dances into the abyss of anarchy.

I cherish the assistance of Prof. G. G. Darah for finding time out of his busy schedules to undertake the task of doing the foreword for this work, Professor Tanure Ojaide for the trouble in wading through the density of my thoughts, Dr. Ebi Yeibo for his inspiring encouragements, and Dr. Stephen Kekeghe for the homely criticism. To my friends, colleagues and the home-front, I say thank you.

Author's Note

The poems in this collection were written in one month, June, 2018. The preceding months were turbulent for Nigeria as a nation: herdsmen and farmers' clashes, Boko Haram insurgence, IPOB (Independent Peoples of Biafra) and the Nigeria military clashes which came to a headway when the latter was proscribed by the Nigerian government as a terrorist group and its leader, Nnamdi Kanu, chased out of the country, as well as inter-court rivalries in different parts of the country.

Boastfully, the Nigerian government had assured all that the country would be self-sufficient in rice and yam productions. In fact, Nigeria has been so self-sufficient in yam production that she now exports them in tons to other parts of the world. Ironically, this is the period the country was under siege by AK47 wielding herdsmen who overran the farmsteads of local farmers in the name of grazing routes. Communities in states such as Benue, Taraba, Adamawa, Kogi, Zamfara, Plateau, Enugu, Nasarawa, Ekiti, Ondo, Edo, Delta, amongst others, were being burnt down by the herdsmen, scores of their citizens killed, while many displaced persons were kept in Internally Displaced People's (IDP) camps. Where then are the farmers to produce the required tons of rice to feed the entire country if they are chased out of their farms and killed?

State governors watched helplessly as their citizens were being slaughtered by faceless herdsmen. In the desperation to protect lives and properties in their domains, many of the governors approached their various houses of Assemblies to enact laws that criminalised open grazing. Of course, it was met with stiff opposition from cattle breeders, under the aegis of Cattle Breeders Association of Nigeria, *Miyetti Allah*. These anti-grazing laws not only triggered further confrontations from the herdsmen who declared open war against such states, but squared such states against the Nigerian government whose idea was for states to donate lands to the herders. The carnage was monumental! In one swoop, over a hundred lives were massacred in Benue state alone, including pregnant women, children, clergy and the elderly. Between January and May, 2018, over a thousand lives were cut down through herdsmen and farmers clashes in different parts of the country.

The Nigerian government, after a 'loud silence', came up with a proposal that every state in the federation should join in the donation of 370,000 hectares of land for cattle colonies as a panacea for a peaceful co-existence between herdsmen and farmers. The proposal was well resisted by the southern part of the country that saw the idea of cattle colony in a country such as Nigeria as not only a misnomer but as another way of internal colonialism. Rather, they suggested ranching as it is done in other parts of the world. Again, this resistance of cattle colonies by the people was met by another round of massacres by Fulani Herdsmen. The Nigerian government, at this point, turned a blind eye to the waves of mindless massacres of its citizens from such states – mainly from the South-South and Christian indigenes of the Middle Belt. The police and the military could not do much. In most cases, they are the tormentors of the people, erecting road blocks of oppression across the land. Mass funeral became a daily routine. The President in one of his broadcasts expressed his helplessness and claimed that the killers were being sponsored by Jihadist groups from Libya, a neighbouring African country!

The people became helpless. Of course, they have been left to die in the hands of strangers by the state. The disillusionment that followed meant that the oppressed peoples of the south lost faith in the Nigerian government. But in order to keep them in check, the Nigeria army had to dance a "python dance" in the eastern part of the country and "crocodile smile" in the south-south region!

Herding South is thus a tribute to the oppressed and dispossessed people of Nigeria who are often the victims of poor leadership and political manoeuvring by the political elite in the country. The poems extend the narrative of dispossession to the internal colonisation that many of the minority groups, especially the people of the Niger Delta suffer in the hands of hegemonic groups in Nigeria. Of course, the leaders of the minority groups are not spared in the existential narrative of the oppressed people of the earth. Truly, the victims of the herdsmen carnage and poor leadership are not only in the IDP camps, but they are in the southern part of Nigeria. They are represented by all the oppressed and dispossessed people of Nigeria, Africa and the entire world. The poems in this collection become the judge of our thoughts and consciences. They are the judge of our actions and inactions as a people who fold their arms or react when the poor and innocent of the land are daily slaughtered and dispossessed of their God-given resources and means of livelihood on the altar of politics, ethnicity and religion.

Peter E. Omoko
November, 2018.

Foreword

Herding South is a collection of poems that explore the multi-bunched crisis of insecurity, crimes of violence and killings by herdsmen, and the oppression and injustice suffered by minority groups in Nigeria. The title of the collection alludes to the pervasive plague of terror, killings, pillage and destruction associated with herdsmen in some northern states of the country. These atrocities have had devastating effect on the agrarian sections of the Middle Belt region. The phrase "herding south" suggests that the marauding groups are bound to extend their mission of destruction to the southern districts of the country. The warning conveyed in the title of the collection encourages the readers to look beyond the bovine economy of cattle rearing to other theatres of insecurity and violence in Nigeria, for example, armed robbery, kidnapping, abduction, and activities of terrorist groups like *boko haram* (education is evil) in the north-east of the country.

The collection is divided into two parts of fifteen poems each. The first part employs the image of the herdsmen and cows to reflect on the worsening situation of turbulence and bloodshed in Nigeria as viewed from the position of the oppressed, poor and neglected majority of the people. In particular, the poet-persona laments the helplessness of the minority nations who suffer violence, death, and loss of property in the hands of blood-thirsty herdsmen and other agents of exploitation. The second part of the collection explores themes relating to the weakness of the victims of oppression and neglect by the ruling elite. The issues raised in *Herding South* are current and urgent; they call for remedial response from the government and wielders of power.

The themes of economics and environment are inter-woven with social and political ones. The nomadic herding of cattle may be a response to dwindling sources of fodder resulting from climate change. Yet, as the poet thinks, this economic need has been exploited and turned into an instrument for raiding and plundering the lands of farming communities. The first poem "The Cow Song" introduces this element; the powers-that-be act as the "drummer" who "supervises the burning carnage/Parading, in full glare, AK47, bearing the/Insignia of national unity". The title poem, "Herding South" is a montage of multiple voices expressed in dramatic dialogue. Like a troubadour, the poet takes us through macabre scenes of death and destruction across the country. The "journey" motif of the narration is apt as it enables us to bear witness to the country-wide spread of insecurity, violence, blood-letting and lamentations. In the midst of these calamities the country's president, who "is a father", makes a broadcast describing the crisis as "a community conflict" about which "There is no cause for alarm."

In failing to disarm and persecute the violent herdsmen, the Nigerian government opens itself to the suspicion of complicity as expressed in the songs of sorrow of people in some Middle Belt states. In the opinion of the poet, "The Middle Belt, already Belted by ceaseless desecration/cries aloud for heaven's vengeance, all hoping/Since the marshland of yams/Of vegetables, of fruits yields its green vegetation/To riffle-carrying cows" This is an allusion to the scenes of massacres witnessed in Benue and other Middle Belt states during invasions by Fulani pastoralists in recent years.

The image of nomadic herdsmen and their cows is familiar in many parts of Nigeria. In the 1960s J. P. Clark wrote a poem titled "Fulani Cattle" in which he marvels at the stoic spirit of the cattle being shepherded by rustic herders from the fringes of the Sahara Desert through the tropical wilds to the "hungry" coastal markets for slaughter. Half a century after, cattle are still being brought south but by herders bearing lethal weapons for aggression, destruction, dispossession and other criminal acts. This is one of the dangers Omoko highlights in the volume.

Herding South is also about oppression, exploitation and injustice. In this context, the poet reminds us of the situation of the minority nations of the Niger Delta of Nigeria whose endowments in oil and gas have fuelled the greed and tyranny of the country's ruling elite for decades. In several poems Omoko laments the impoverished condition of the masses of the region, blaming it partly on their docility and the corruption of political elite. The poet adorns the voice of the griot and sings "...to spite the scorpion that vacates/Its rocky throne to forage in the marshland of ants" The poet is "drunk with the problems of the land" his "tongue is vexed with vibrant blood/To sing with stones and clubs". In the poem titled "The Command" Omoko employs a mock-heroic tone to refer to Abuja-based tyrants as "General killer-killer" who marches "into the creeks to spread terror" so that "My crude oil must continue to flow/My petro-dollar vault must not die in shame". General killer-killer orders troops thus: "March into the creeks with your squad of terror/Let your guns cough out the dark smoke of death/Across the thighs of their rivers.../Spread the garment of terror in their hearts.." With these belligerent words, the Abuja rulers use "crocodile dance" and "smart tricks of politics" to subjugate the Niger Delta. In other poems, Omoko deploys his angst against the comprador elite of the region as evident in "The Battle Within", "A Song of Memory" "The Bunkering Song" and "Who Them Help?"

The currency of the themes of the poems will endear them to diverse audiences and cultures. But the beauty of the collection also comes from the fluid, free-flowing verse and modes of narration. In many pieces the poet's moral outrage fuses elegantly with the sing-song flourish of the lines. This aesthetic feature derives from the works of J. P. Clark, the inimitable master of Nigerian poetry in English expression. Besides Clark, Omoko has also benefited from the radical outlook and poetic craft of the generation of Niyi Osundare, Tanure Ojaide, Odia Ofeimun, Ezenwa-Ohaeto, Ogaga Ifowodo, Obari Gomba, Ebinyo Ogbowei and Ebi Yeibo. With several published plays, Omoko has shown his creative talents as a dramatist; this debut collection of poems signals his potential as a singer of tales.

G. G. Darah
Warri, 2019

I

Some dewdrop clings to the eyes
However hard we shake the head

– **Tanure Ojaide**

I have experienced a baffling matter
Listeners, lend me your ears
It is narration that expands an idea
Bread soaked in water loses value
Men of great wealth we have extolled in song
Now it is the turn of philosophical issues
An attentive student does well in exams.

– **Sir Juju/Udjabor**

Contents

Dedication
Acknowledgements
Author's Note
Foreword

I

The Cow Song - 1
This Nigeria Sef - 2
How They Tricked Us - 5
The Naïve Peace - 6
Herding South - 8
The Hunter Goes Berserk - 15
Wailing the Herdsman's Flute - 17
They Call Me Restive - 19
Ominous Silence - 20
Some Have Walked This Path Before - 21
The Dancing Cloud - 22
I Love my President - 24
The Village Square is Empty - 27
The Clan Song - 30
The Command - 31

II

Prayers - 33

A Song of Memory - 36
The Night Sings a Song - 37
The Battle Within - 39
The Questioner - 40
The Emperor in the Ivory Tower - 49
The Flames of Our Blood - 50
The Cast Away - 51
The Bunkering Song - 52
The Day Papa Tip-toed into the Night - 54
Ghost Dance - 56
Mourners - 58
Our Crime - 59
Cast a Spell - 60
Who Dem Help? - 61

Glossary - 63

The Cow Song

I am intoxicated with the pains of the land
Let me sing till night comes to
Sedate my eyes with sleep
The rich speak wisdom into the heads of their
Wards to perpetuate their greed in the inner chambers
The poor man's child hears of wisdom
Only from the lips of the wind
I will sing to spite the scorpion that vacates
Its rocky throne to forage in the marshland of ants
I will dance without restraint
Let passersby laugh at my nakedness
Let their lips kiss my past
The sun may set, dusk may creep in
The earth remains firm in its stead

I am drunk with the problems of the land
And now my tongue is vexed with vibrant blood
To sing with stones and clubs, decapitating
The gay-gatherings of death
Shrivelled cows, tired of desert turf, sway
In lunatic greed to devour without restraint
The sweat of a year-long devotion
Royal cows mow without contemplation, and
Dance to the death of scented farmlands
Around the courtyard, swathing misery on
The teeth of tender cassavas

Dewdrops drift, cascading raffia palms while
Morbid grasses are strewn in the rumen of darkness
The drummer supervises the burning carnage,
Parading, in full glare, AK47, bearing the
Insignia of national unity
That man may die for cow to live

This Nigeria Sef
(On the way to the airport from Eko Hotel
with Prof Dul Johnson and Diran Ademiju-Bepo)

Tell us
The mosquitoes that infested us
With filarial parasites that our nation's feet
Drag, burdened with elephantiasis
Sunk to the ground in retardation

We cry of capital flight
Of hospitality demons from Lebanon
And South Africa that enjoy the wealth
Of our government and oil companies
With mangled history of noisome luxury,
An elusive cockpit, passed through fangled cunts
Wetted with lemonade on beds,
On pearls that clamp our feet to the
Ground in faded fancy

We jerked and foamed our mouths out
When at the restaurant downstairs
Children of political brats peck on food
And Growl on expensive wine,
Earpieces tucked on their heads
Hands folded on faded jeans,
Sagged to the knees,
Exchanging room keys for meal tickets
For eating nothing

We all looked from our hotel rooms
Spellbound by the forest of high-rise buildings
Sprawling through Victoria Island
The lagoon that stretched its feet like
Octopus into the distance,

The galaxy of cars that convey demi-gods
Who curse the feet of the reception desk
Bearing letters of recommendation from
Overfed spirits, drunken by the smell of
Crude oil, piped from the arteries
Of the Niger Delta

Why can't this coffee-street
Of cultured roads
Of snaking bridges
Of high-rise buildings fetter the soil
Of the Niger Delta if it is true
That the Nigeria greedy stomach
Is fed, daily from the crude oil and gas
In their sea and farmlands?
I had thought, aloud

The replies were instantaneous,
Shooting from both sides in staccato speed
As if predetermined:
'Ask your leaders',
'What have they done with their 13%?'

Kweke*!
What has one's leader got to do
With a distress cry coated in bright ribbons?
What has one's leader got to do
With the choking cry of a child
Whose yam has been taken from him
By an ogre that seeks death in place
Of restitution?

Kweke!
Will you not cry
When mortals pull rough string

Herding South

On the neck of the rivers that
The fishes may die?
If 13% is purged on the fangled rings
Of naked earth,
Vomited on the shrivelled thighs
Of the Niger Delta,
Won't it take eternity for it to laugh
Like civilised brats of Victorian Island?
Didn't you take 1% of Nigeria's
Annual budget to feed the greedy
Appetite of Abuja that it now
Sits in thrones with foreign diplomats?

Or has Nigeria cut out the head
Of the clans
That no one ever remembers
The truce of independence
In the endless dance of
National interest of
Meals taken away from a child to
Feed an adult?

How They Tricked Us

Is my country not funny?
They will award contracts
Directly for the development
Of their stomach
And build bridges of
Unity in the north
But when it gets to
The Niger Delta,
After they have drunk
The crude oil to their fill
And farted away all
The natural gas,
They will hold meetings
To clear the rivers
Of water hyacinth
They will set up
Commissions to brush
The teeth of the dispossessed
Squirrels and create ministry
Of Niger Delta Affairs
To serve them more food

The Naïve Peace

Herdsmen bumped into my farmstead,
Cut open the throats of my companions

But my man only stares
At naked breasts of decapitated bodies

Bushmen, in great passion,
Swaggered menacingly into my home
Stepped on pots and smashed my plates
Against the muddy walls

But my man only prays
That they go in peace

Strangers tied me down,
Lunged at me, hitting my buttocks
With their stinking things

But my man only reels in bitter laughter,
Praying that the intruders
Are not offended, as it were,
To leave with my life

Not done,
They went into my kitchen,
In rapid sequence,
Ate up my grains,
And set it on fire

Yet my man dodges eye contact
With me, fretting at the dust
Of fleeing rodents

Then I carried the burning tears
In my eyes and poured it
On the feet of the clan;
The fat men there belched fire
In fierce arrogance and called me witch,
The very daughter of *Eshu*,*
Sent to the clan,
To dry up their fat stomachs
Shrivelled folks, abandoned in the ruins
Of hunger, swallowed their tongues
Until they coughed blood and died

Now, Bushmen grew wings
And dug roots in my farmstead,
Erecting slumming quarters
Where they collect 'ground money' from me

Then, I bore my pains on my back,
Crossing six streams, south-south the land
But no one put a consoling hand
Around my shoulder,
None wiped the deluge of tears in my eyes

Who,
    Then,
        Shall give ears
            To this ominous tale
                Of herders,
                    Herding south?

Herding South

           I
What have we made of our lives
That we choose in turns, mountains of pains,
Whitewashed on the head of the clan,
Spewed-red in a torrent of slit throats?
Herders heading south in
Un-courted rage to
Enforce the craze of countless colonies
Spread wide on the lips of cattle owners
In the throne of power:
Desert gods who seek shelter in
The forest sinews of the south
Once scored by experts as
Cursed habitat of tsetse fly;
Deadly daemon that sells trypanosomiasis as
Wares to cows!

The ululation of mega-corruption,
Selected from a heap of files of freak hyenas
Floats in the midst of morbid hyacinth
Through pathways of wasteland,
Down waterways, from the high to the low
The ancient emperor must bring down
Trees not pieced together in the mesh of
Terror on the clan
How else can the rhythm of century-long, be
Rehearsed across the land,
If it is not hidden in the fingers of cattle colonies
When the tonalities of ranches
Enchant the world of civilised climes?

           II

The Middle, already Belted by ceaseless desecration,
Cries aloud for heaven's vengeance, all hoping
Since the marshland of yams,
Of vegetables, of fruits yield its green vegetation
To riffle carrying cows
The remains of a jihad long lost
In the drums of cricket tales,
Inscribed in primal shelves of the
Country's lore of valour, of
Tribes who held together their ground
Against blood thirsty jihadists, centuries earlier

The wind sings her cricket tale of
Overloaded grief, wrought on innocent
Children and women by a reign of terror,
Encased in assorted dumbness of progressive shit
Who rub in all, the pomade of ancient misery
The raised dust of imperialism
Indeed, a fearless proposal on
A clan of elegant tongues

III

They gather like flies
Upon broken bones on spirit ridges
To court the soul of the south
Languid elders that lost their deaths,
Many years ago in the pot of death
Smashed against their jaws
When khaki men wear perfumes
For a group photograph of victory
That kept the clan together
How do you steal from a child
Yet stops him from crying?
But they sit again to apportion grasslands

Herding South

To foster friendship long lost
In the frosty current that cascade the south

IV

The moon sulks as the cloud spews salty tears
That rain beyond river Benue or Niger
Billion stars closed their eyes
As royal cattle overrun the streets,
Farmlands and homes
Bearing certificates of occupancy
The herders are assured and resolute
Casting sickles and machetes on open necks

The terrain is no longer a fault
Cows wade into muddy swamps in gusto,
Waddle in mangled streams,
Clamping their teeth on lazy twigs
They slap the luxuriant elephant grass
And erect tents on the ridge of pumpkin leaves
Where they regurgitate the chaffs of yam tendrils
The herders are assured and resolute
Casting sickles and machetes on open necks

Pigs are no longer religious taboos,
They even eat the entrails of snails
It is the man that takes alcohol
That it intoxicates
The head must be exorcised for the
Cleansing ritual of darkness and death
Cows are the bargainers,
The heir to a glorious estate
Conquered in a sworn oath
They lash on shrivelled ears of cassava,
Draped by overuse potheads
Of polluted mash lands
The only inheritance of an inherited wife

Passed on, to remain in the clan
Bruised fingers and bruised feet
Scours death in the dark of night
Of sliced throats
Of strayed brat
Of rippled stomach
Of pregnant mothers
Of blind bath
To the shame of all

V

At sunrise,
Mmm, sunrise!
After the marauders have harvested
The souls of the clan,
A dusk to dawn curfew of deceit is
Vomited in the airwaves
For the charred bodies of rage
Deserve a homily funeral in mass
Where dossiers of deaths are compared,
Regime by regime to the buzz of dragonflies

In the night of carnage,
The deluge of charred bodies
Break the records, drifting
From hundreds to thousands
Depending on the media
Where dossiers of deaths are compared,
Regime by regime to the buzz of dragonflies

Our land knows not the taste of
Hurricane, cyclone or tornadoes
We would have summoned *Aziza** to placate
Their anger with deadly winds

Herding South

Nor did we boast of earthquake
That swallows the bones and homes
Of the west, for the gods
Know that our plate eats
The toil of the ground
Yet they plague us with human disasters –
Where dossiers of deaths are compared,
Regime by regime to the buzz of dragonflies

Last night,
After shedding the tears of grudge
To scorn the gash in the naked head of children
The emperor gawks,
He was not told his police chief
Did not sleep in the wilderness of slaughter
Yet at a state banquet
The emperor smiles to the
Amazement of all;
A tab in hand,
Admiring the herd of cows
Whitened by the blood
Of innocent children
Cut open, the night earlier

VI

Mr. Iortom, he has lost
His wife and five children
To the colony of cattle rustlers
Their lives cut short –
In a rite of passage, tucked in rattled guts
Like a sailor, disposing the chaff of
A cigarette on a canoe carrying
Mats and a keg of fuel
Their charred bodies are carried
In wheelbarrows,

Weaving tale of cranky dirge
Of egrets banished from seashore
By greedy crocodiles
The clan, already barred from bathing
Their dead stand, nodding dizzy heads
To the scorn of seated sorrows of unkempt pubic
It is the rhythm of the cattle dance:
'Never let the native get close to their dead,
The exact figure maybe coughed out
To exorcise blood reddened for war'

Five or six soldiers took charge
Of the funeral mass, amassing the dead
In a mass grave –

'I know that man,' chorused Iortom
In a voice betraying grief and triumph
When the body of his pastor,
Hacked in two halves
Sank into the shallow mass grave
The bones of children,
Flapping necks of pregnant mothers
Picked from the craggy grass,
Dotted with the memory of blood
Crank together in one grave,
Massed together in a funeral mass
As *Miyetti-Allah** spokesperson claps
To the sky, clanking the sour blood
Clamped in the bulging hearts of those alive:
'More souls will die
If you don't donate your lands
For our grazing rights'

VII

Truly, the president is a father
His 'mourning' broadcast after many
Weeks of mock silence, divides
The sense of exhausted mermaids
That morning, tides refused to flow
Monkeys refused to eat luscious bananas
Thrown at them, herons cut
Companies with cows bleached
White with the blood of the clan

'It is a communal conflict,' he had said
In a mournful swag, his genuine pains
Flowed out of his gold-coated goggle
Like a vexed dam emptied on the thighs
Of shrivelled farmsteads:
'There is no cause for alarm,
It is a case of two-fighting without
A third party to separate them.'
Who has ever seen the cricket carry
Its young on its back?

'My government is committed to protecting
Lives and properties,' he continued
Whether from his nose or from his mouth,
No one ever doubted his commitments
To put cows in the homes of every citizen
By twenty-nineteen,
Campaign promises kept.

The Hunter Goes Berserk

The hunter goes into the forest,
All night long,
Waging immortal war with mosquitoes
But returns to the village square
With an empty bag
His eyes sludge in the biting rays of dawn
Only to find the arena covered in the lush of festivity
Maidens bare their breasts to the secret of the light
Their waists, decorated with beads,
Swerved to the winds in vibrated hysteria
The drummers curdle their drums and
Let loose the bewitched rhythms that
Brought out the blue that once lights our sky
When the teeth are happy, they laugh

But the hunter fears the peering eyes of spectators
Every herb is useful to the ant
In rage, he runs into the homes of his kinsmen
And decimated their bones,
Like one drunk with the blood of injustice
He turns against the spectators;
And packs their bones into a crate
In a rite to spite the clan

The dancers went berserk,
Leaving their breast to dangle in rage;
Left, right,
Left and right
In a python dance in the east
Crocodile smiles to the creeks
As the warthog leads the way for zombies to follow
brandishing gunboats on finless butterfly

The spirit takes hold of the recalcitrant hunter,
Letting out foams from his mouth,
He marches in swift precision:
Left, right,
Left and right
In a python dance in the east
That summons the towncrier,
Grandson of Lucifer,
Christened Lai on the nineteenth day
Of the year of our Lord,
To spread the gory tale of valour

The dog wags its tail,
Taunting the despoiled sea to the sky
It is what one is adept in
That he lives by
Sai Baba!
The husky voice from the savannah
Chorused, as the lanky emperor mounts
The throne to supervise the
Final burial of the clan

Peter Omoko

Wailing the Herdsman's Flute

Memory may fail,
But I have searched the gauntlet,
Behold the precipice and I am sure
Of the hunter who snaps the life out of
The mouth of the talking drum

The marauder cuts down forests to spite
The grass, his hands drip with the blood of boast

The hunter hunts not for game to earn
The cheering drums of gazelles,
He kills to spite the blood of the clan
His fingers ooze from the smells of hatred;
A forerunner of wobbled jihad
As he sneers on whacked nerves of disabled farmers

The marauder cuts down forests to spite
The grass, his hands drip with the blood of boast

The herdsman scavenges in the farm owner's grave
Because his drummers sit in power
In a victory party
That chokes the wind to death.

The marauder cuts down forests to spite
The grass, his hands dripped with the blood of boast

And so,
The herdsman slaughters uncountable farmers
To atone the life of a missing calf;
He sacks a sleeping clan to toast the recovery
Of a wounded calf –

Herding South

The marauder cuts down forests to spite
The grass, his hands drip with the blood of boast

But everyday,
The mound of slain women and children
Rain curses on a world that drowns the calabash –

They call Me Restive

You call me restive
For asking to be equal with you
Despite the assortments in my pot

I call you thief
For taking what belongs to me
To increase your size

Do you not see the ridge of your mouth,
Woven into the artery of greed,
Swallowing the stars of the sky?

Yet you call me restive
For asking to be equal with you
When you seized what belongs to me

I shall come to you with clubs, cudgels,
And machetes to slice away that you've
Taken from me that we may be equal

Ominous Silence

What clairvoyant
Silenced the drum of the people's activist
That marabouts sleep-walk
In dotted corners
As clouds, dark and mean
Chased away into the conundrum –
The naked breasts of justice
Knocked down by grim powers!

*Babalawos** retreat
None could recite the arid verses
Chained in the faded cowries of *Ifa**
For the cobweb is thick
Pressing hard on the shoulder
Of onlookers dazed by the
Daylight robbery of the clan's voice
In the ditty of next level

The drum of the Avengers
Has certainly eaten rotten yam pudding
On the tarmac of greed
What god condones sacrilege
In the altar of worship?

Perhaps a little prompting
Is all the wind needs
To MEND the land
Before the sea part ways
On the threshold of
Okigbo's thunder!

Some Have Walked This Path Before

Now that the sun is still standing in the sky
The rivers yet ebb and flow
Through the recesses of some sane minds
And the storm slowly growl,
Poked and teased by the echoing
Voices of broken bones
Let the woods be gathered from the ruins

True,
Some have walked this path before
The slayers, fugitives and damned wanderers
Companions to wayward wanderers
Wandering South

And some have worn this damned robes before
But here they hung their hatred
In their machetes and daggers
Passionless nomad,
Weaned from infant
To mindless slayers
Haunting the toils of the clan

The raindrops opened old scars
Of the mind, wacked together
In the head of senile ghosts
In a barren ante-room
Drained out to the west of opaque dwellings
Where walls of ineptitude crashed in time

The Dancing Cloud

Dark cloud danced
In red communion of treason
Dancing menacingly at unyielding homestead
With human heads tied on crushed staff

Dark cloud danced
In the sky, on mountain tops,
On tree branches and then crashes on
The shoulders of market women,
Jobless youths and hopeless fathers

Human flesh strewn the land in
The race for power, as
The election fire chokes the child in the womb
Twenty thousand and nineteen times
Rigging the soul of the clan in cold blood

Dark cloud danced
On the nation's head as
Corruption files spread their legs apart,
Warning tribunal gods against the sight
Of sacrificial food at the crossroads
But when the greedy eat they also pay
Homage to the size of the toilet
Judge judging judge in a communal ritual
After a DSS raid that lasted all night
In barefaced murder of the law

Dark cloud danced
To shame the law
Of one party cut into two by greed
Of moon and cloud dancing to spite the sky
The sun smiling its heart away

Casting ominous rays at men who
Drag sluggishly like sliming mullets
Gasping for breath in the floor of
Oloibiri's* bleeding canoe

Dark cloud danced
In the air, spreading AK47 as a wreath
In honour of the dead, taunting
The consciences of all
In an election fire that killed
The child in the womb
Twenty thousand and nineteen times

I Love My President

I love
My President
And my President
Loves me too
He swore to protect
My life and properties
If I vote him into power
And so he campaigned to my house

That day,
He spoke in the English language
We both understand
That day,
I entrusted my life
And properties in his care

Those who knew him
As an upright man,
Warned me to be weary
Of his wild joke,
I only winked and laughed
At their folly

So the day
He was announced
As my President,
I emptied two gallons
Of palm wine and
Trekked from my village
To congratulate him in
*Aso-Rock**

There,
I met patriotic baboons who swore
They loved him more
And can die for his ignorance
I only winked and laughed
At their folly

The witches and wizards
In my village laughed at me,
Swearing, he is their member
And the chief of mischief
I only winked and laughed
At their folly

Soon
He settled into power
The rains came
And flooded his head
He forgot the promise
He made to me
And when cattle came,
Ate up my crops,
And defecated in my home,
I cried aloud,
The police came and
Recorded my speech
The following day,
Cattle rustlers came,
Burnt down my house
And left with the souls
Of my village

Then I cried louder
My lovely president came
After a meeting with his security

Herding South

Chiefs, all members of his clan
Where they spoke
The language of his birth
That is unknown to me,
He came to my village,
Steadied his gold-plated goggle
Casting a benign smile at
The decapitated bodies of children
He patted my back and
Assured me that my
Loses are in the interest
Of the nation!

The Village Square is Empty

The singers are bemused to
Find the village square empty
The poisoned fumes they carry in
Their mouth is like a pestilence that
Eats the child in the womb unknown
To the careless mother

Oh, the village square is empty
Birds fly in opposite directions, ears bar
From the cacophonic rhythms
Virgins are abroad, dangling angered breasts
But monkeys closed their
Eyes to livid obscenities
How does excrement find
Its way into the moustache!

My Lai is done telling lies
The marketplace is empty
Even dragon flies refused to buzz around
The shit Lai carries in his mouth
Worms creep out of his stomach
Fearing being choked to death
By the stench of his lies

Oh, the marketplace is empty
The deluge of lies that sit in Lai's mouth
Are not lullabies to sooth the
Hymens of simple hearts
Lunatics eat the lies from empty heads
Now they are congealed in Lai's gullet
Swearing to hold him accountable

Herding South

Our Ogbe is tired of memorising idiotic lines
The street is deserted
Masked lines, couched in fear and murder
Loose lines that mock the tortoise's back

Oh, the street is deserted
His Nigeria-made rice are bagged
In foreign sacks
Enacted to mock the world
His imported Brazilian grasses only
Feed strayed Aso-Rock cows
His exported yams have bent the backs
Of the Benue's clans

All hail to the Minister of blood!
He plunges the Plateau into the ominous
Machine guns of herdsmen

All hail to the Minister of blood!
The bones of his Zamfara rice farmers are
Dismantled and crushed

All hail to the Minister of blood!
The homes of his Taraba fruit farmers are
Drenched in the blood of betrayal

All hail to the Minister of blood!
The homes of his Benue yam farmers are
Raped and razed to ashes by bare-feet nomads
Whose brains abhor the sight of buildings
The birds are in flight, barring their ears
From the inanities of the prodigal

The courts are empty
Shaming pampered SANs, morbid
Crickets that fire darts of disgrace
The court is the marketplace for illegal heresies
To court the goodwill of the state

Sagay cries rooftops to mock fecund statesmen
Whose licentious greed greets
The nose with gracious stench
The cannons of his wigs flay the rule of law,
The creed that sedates his luscious career
To uphold national interests of serfs
The balm for tyrant dance

Falana hangs his wig on a pendulum
To dance the dance of the spirit:
"Seduce me", the spirit urges
"I will dance to debase the law", he replies
Mocking the truce that binds the clan together
The delirium works in all when
The kindred spirits desert the homestead

Keyamo taunts the monkeys
That held back his SANship for years
Howling stones and venoms
The singers must sing
Even if the village square is empty

The Clan Song

Every season of draught
Empties our hopes
Into this cage of stayed laughter
As the clan marsh out for the routine
Drink of sour grapes,
Staring at faces – paled and
Drenched on the shadows of wailings
Eyeing death from the head to the toe
Above the statutory ritual of passage
Where we all eat dusts from empty pots,
Hoping, hoping one day,
The hyenas will fall down and die
In this vaguely packed carapace of death
Herding south, strong and mean

Cries and wailings do not go
To the battlefield to receive medals.
Lead the way, let's speak the language
Of return and tuck needles in their boots,
Piercing them with discomfort in the head
Heap *egbesu* *poison in their teacups
That in the passion of their greed,
They would swallow anguish and pain

The Command

'General killer-killer
March into the creeks with your
Squad of terror
And dance the crocodile ditty
Rehearsed at the last security party
Drink the blood of any ant that
Crosses your path in protest of the fart of my greed
My crude oil must continue to flow
My petrol-dollar vault must not die in shame
Must it be my days that their god's vision
Will speak of justice and equity?
Were they asleep when we signed
Their future into our palms?

March into the creeks with your squad of terror
Let your guns cough out the dark smoke of death
Across the thighs of their rivers
Beat your drums loud that owls may flap
Their wings to despoil their deadly darts
Spread the garment of terror in their heart
That they may become spineless
Let your crocodile dance
Shame the skirt of rejected gods
Knocked down by smart tricks of politics.'

II

Each society is concerned with its destiny within the cosmic arena. Without this perspective, the society can only be stampeded into directions it does not fully comprehend or does not feel ready to follow.
— **Mazisi Kunene**

It is seeing and not talking that swells the jaws
— **Urhobo proverbs**

Prayers

Do not turn your back on us
Guardian spirits,
Attend to our supplications
Take kola nuts
Take a sip from our drink
Do not reject our farina
Garnished with palm-oil

May the staring sky bear witness!

Our land once bloomed with petals of laughter
The rivers rub their skin on little children,
Stripped naked in playful glee
Creeks spread their brackish skin
To cover little tilapias and crayfish
In their herd, attending meetings with fearful
Barracudas in our nets
The trees dance *egbada** when the wind
Storms the forest in a dance duel
The rains visit the clan in season
To serve the earth its portion of drink
That the eyes of cassava and watermelon may sprout

May the staring sky bear witness!

Our farmlands sit on oil wells
They say our earth carries a sea
Of natural gas to light up our world
We will be rich, our youths cry
Raising impatient hands to greet your benevolence
The winds sway in ecstatic swagger
We all laughed and danced to

Your altar to offer prayers

May the staring sky bear witness!

Many tides have passed
Age has conferred on us the status of seers
But no one could remember
The maiden's songs
The mighty iroko trees are
Disappearing from the forest
Our rivers now spread their brackish
Linen with oily blood
Khaki men now roam our land
They sit on gunboats as diadem of terror,
Wading machine guns on monkeys and squirrels
The crude oil that sits in our farmlands is
Now a bloc owned by traders in faraway lands
The rains only cough fever and diarrhoea
The sun infects us with cancer and bronchitis
We are now rabbits hunted down
By those we call brothers
We all cried!

The staring sky has been our witness!

Do not turn your back on us
Our ancestors
Attend to our supplications
Take kola nuts,
Take a sip from our drink
That we may eat and forget our sorrows
Do not reject our farina
Garnished with palm-oil
May our creeks be fertile
That our nets be heavy with fish

Keep away crabs from our nets
We desire bountiful harvest
Grant us good health and may
Our days be prolonged
May those who come to drill crude oil
From our land remember us the owners
The oil company cannot light up its yards,
Day and night while we remain in darkness
Let the same pipe they use in
Ferrying our crude oil to distant lands
Be used to bring good water to quench our thirst
May our children be managers and directors
In the oil companies
We are the owners of the land,
The oil wells too.

The staring sky has been our witness

Take mashed yam,
Take unripe plantain
May the fragrance of the powder
Incite you to rage
That our oppressors be stung with strange ailments
If the bottle is not turned upside down,
The drunk will not be pacified
Guardian spirits,
Attend to our supplications
That we may laugh again
And renew our vows to pay you
Yearly homage

A Song of Memory

I weave my tales into songs
To enchant the heart of passersby
The parrot is born a wordsmith
Who can deny it?
The tale of the poor only amuses
Royal throne of greed, as the
Blood of fowls smeared on lifeless idols
Those who said I cannot sing
Let them hear my song
And dance without restraint

I will sing to bug the memory of all
Daring to embarrass those who drink
With our cups but thank us
With the pieces of its smashed remains
May my muse lift my tongue to
Mountain tops that recalcitrant trees
May dance for their fruits to fall

My fishing nets have seen little tides
Since the arrival of the lifeless emperor
Who drinks natural gas like pepper soup
In motor park bars, and mortgage our crude oil in
The thighs of Chinese loans, as his tiny
Stomach drags about in mournful fancy

The land is brain-sick to my plight
For, in every corner of the world,
My beauty makes headlines, yet in my land
They cough blood to blanket my dreams

The Night Sings a Song

Last night,
The maidens refused to dance
The lofty steps that stir
The heart of brave youths
The stilt dancers break their revelled sticks
Before the peering eyes of alien gods
To shame the clan
The earth parts ways, pouring out testaments of
Rage into the ears of drifting chiefs
Who eat today that tomorrow may die

Last night,
The canoe capsized,
And the clan broke with a snap
Each clinching to tongue-line and parasol of faith:
That nectar of hate transported from
Alien shores at the crossroad,
Where the wind disperses to our earth
The crude vermin of our uncivilisation

Last night,
Fleets of gunboats,
Strapped with machine guns, came,
Seeking the death of anyone daring to
Stop the country, faraway from shore,
From arrogating the oil and gas communion
Of a clan to itself
Crocodiles strolled under roots, abandoning
Creeks that once wet the fang of their teeth
With seasoned cuisines, all moon
Hyacinths made way for their perilous transits,
Sea-currents labour wearily to

Herding South

Hunt down their propellers of doom, sent
To conquer the voice of the clan
In a rite of blood on crude oil
That enacts our strange history

Today,
Dawn knocks at the door
Beaming with smiles as
The cloud escorts the sun
To take its throne in the sky where
The creeks and forests will laugh again

The Battle Within

Because we'd fight
The dog fight when we eat
The food left us by grandfather,
You went to the village square
And invited strangers to take away the pot
When they serve us spoonful of garbage
To satisfy our thirst
You cry of being robbed

The Questioner

Group: Oh, our son, *te bra o*!
    Do you still eat farina and roasted
    Iced fish like us in this murky marshland?

Solo: Of course! Was I not born here?
    The crocodile gives birth to its kind, teeth
    And rapacious appetite in these frozen creeks
    Tamara* is my witness, my umbilical cord was buried
    Beside the root of that mahogany tree over there
    I bathed in the fangled and polluted rivers of the Niger Delta
    I walked in the muddy sinews of Otuoke,
    Pantless, bare-feet, swollen with worm's torments

Group: Oho! So you remembered those days?

Solo: Ah those days! When monkeys danced on our rooftops
    To mock at our nakedness,
    Our teeth bruised and bled at the sight of *akoro**,
    Its chaff kept the root of our teeth strong as
    Men of the Niger Delta
    Those were the days when each tide
    Came with its own gifts
    Maidens danced without restraint and charged
    The village square with bare breasts,
    And men were born

Group: Oh, *Ayuba**! Your son is not lost after all
    Our son, what then blurred your memory
    That you allow the government to force faeces into
    Our throats when you drank the fresh water of other
        worlds?

Solo: Blur my memory? Am I not the son of a canoe maker?
    Of mighty mahogany, paddled in raft,
    Through the huge brackish belly of Amabo creeks,
    Up to the sunny shelves of Owei camp,
    By the side of the forest where Arogbo folks
    Fall face-down before the huge basket of fish
    From the Urhobo side, bolstering with burning tales?
    The sun throws its rays into the air like
    Daggers that pierce the back of grandpa as
    He chisels the skin of a dug-out log
    Before it is corked with palm nut chaffs
    And the spark of fire that burn all night
    Twilight wove its tale at all
    Until the young white priest came and taught
    Us how to recite their hymns
    I never liked it, but was fascinated at his knowledge
    Of the forests and wetlands of the deltas –
    He called leopard by its name,
    Named each fish that clung to our net and
    Sang with birds under trimmed trees
    The tides came and sucked the feet of
    Our camp, spreading its arms across the thighs
    Of thatched huts, belching cold and fever
    That night, grandpa snapped us from the surge
    His big canoe steaming through water hyacinth
    As we backed the haggling flood in slow motion
    I was mid adult and lost

Group: Oh, you remembered it all!
    But you left for the city and cleaned us white
    Like chickens and plantain, waiting to be cast
    Into abyss; the white men came with their companies,
    To drill our blood like morning breeze allotted for our
        funerals
    The government came with their laws that tied

Herding South

Our hands backward, axe above our heads,
Snaking down in fury to cut the throat of any egret
That pecks close to its feet, swollen with greed and
    blood

You left for the city, crawling in palaces
Where the tide of Aghoro river became a curse
Broken to free your feet, shod in the salty waters
Of the deltas; the tide ebbs and full, several seasons
And your footsteps died in the belly of the creeks
A child never forgets his father's name
But you did! You even cursed the breast of Tamara
That gave you life. Ayuba, your son left us,
He ran away, eyes closed like Oedipus*
Chased away from his clan by the curse of the gods

Solo: I did not run away like some
    Butterflies afraid of becoming birds
    I only scrambled to know our parts
    The forest of the deltas had enchanted me,
    The rivers are my blood, flowing through the
    Recesses of my veins, as I sought knowledge in books,
    Bearing fruits and wallowing drudgingly like
    Millipede, heavy with the pains of the clan,
    I could name the birds by my fingers in the
    Whiteman's tongue; the fishes and animals in
    Our forests yield their names to me like Adam*
    In Eden; I mocked the names of plants from
    Toru-Orua to the fortress of Tẹbẹsọnọma* of the Seven
Heads,
    I danced like a prince, fearless and strong
    And they came and pierced on my chest, a Ph.D – a
    True son of *mein**, a rising sun,
    Unshaved with the burden of the sea

Group: True! We all cried to Owei in jubilation!

And then the speedboats came that anxious morning,
Cutting through the arteries of fangled water hyacinth
With their ominous propellers, mangrove trees waving
At them on both sides as they touched ground in the
Muddy altar of Amabolowei, starved by naked
    worshippers,
Shrivelled in poverty, but the clan was fearless,
One by one they all came out, the brave first
And then the women beater:
'We need one of your sons with plenty of book wisdom
To dance with us in government house
To beautify the bride of the land,' the big chief chorused!
The words stung our ears like thunder, trusting its fire
Into our blood, reddened with joy
The birds carried it in tonalities and the winds
Dispatched it to each household, near and far
That was how you were chosen above us,
The true sons of Otuoke to pour libation on our
Behalf in government house
We did not grudge but processed like herders herding
    south
To the altar of Amabolowei to sacrifice on your behalf
May Ayuba bear witness!

Solo: That is true my kinsmen
    Fresh plantain anchored in the community pot
    With each household pledging a chicken or a plate of
        farina
    And the clan danced the day I wore the robe of politics
    I did not let you down,
    May Ayuba bear witness!

    I fought side by side with the Governor-General
    Of our people in taming the flood that comes
    To eat our homes every full moon

In our arms, Bayelsa State was born and
Nurtured like a cold current in full-tide
Our love for the land knows no bounds
Throttling through Rivers and Delta in infinite
Spirit, we sang the thunder song that sends
Thieving generals into hiding, 'resource control,
Me I no go tire,' billowed in the air and it
Crushed the stone-heart of the hawk,
It choked until it coughed out thirteen percent
Of our blood, stalked away in its hundred-rooms
    mansion

The Governor-General danced that night without
    restraint
Knotting in one swoop, the beards of the
Thieves who have drilled the fangled crude oil
Of our land, he blocked the doorways against those
In Aso Rock who flogged our backs and stole our crude
    oil
To light up other climes

The Governor-General danced without restraint,
The dancers stopped dancing but he surged ahead,
Playing his own rhythm of death
At dawn, he had seized the mythic wand in
Drunken ecstasy from the masquerade,
That day, he died!
I was called,
Hands tied backward,
To dress his funeral bed!

Group: Dried meat stick in your teeth, our son,
    The river flowed backward,
    The rains held back its greasy tears
    From our land the day you dressed
    His funeral bed,

Amabolowei's altar caved-in and the sea
Swallowed up our offerings
The day you connived with thieving merchant
And betrayed the clan
May Ayuba bear witness!

The day the Governor-General was disgraced
In foreign markets, you added petrol to
The already burning furnace
Mermaids left seashore in shame,
We the women of Bayelsa, bared our breasts
To curse thieving sons who hide in the shadow
Of our poverty to defraud us
But when the Governor-General in fierce
Arrogance, returned to reclaim his throne,
You were fast to use his men against him and
Out-laughed the game, forcing your toe
Into the fleshy spine of the delta
And you fleeced our world to its death

Of course, it earned you the applause of the
Ragged masquerade, you drank champagne
In his bedroom at Abeokuta and ate the
Blood of roasted pig with him in Aso-Rock
You find your way into his heart
But the clan wail,
May Ayuba bear witness!

Solo: Was it not how I became his pet dog,
And you celebrated to the rooftops?
If I failed the clan, you too must share in the blame
Oh yes! You too must share in the blame
You cheered me on!
No one reminded me that I was dancing naked
When it earned me, first, the Vice President,

And then the President, you cheered me on!
The boys threw their guns in the creeks to
Support my nibbled legs and dragged my hands
Until I sat on the seat that mangled
Our lives in the Niger Delta

We thought it was a feast without end
But our oppressors are wise
They brought their own drummers
And danced naked to rob tears in the face of the earth
They tied a leash on my waist
So that the day I try to move forward,
They'll drag it backward,
In that orgy for thirst for blood,
The devil, dressed in boko-haram*
Let loose its slaughter knife,
It transverses the boundary of peasant farmers
And climbs into the precincts of homily
Cutting the throats of worshippers
In that twirling morning mass of May,
Yet you cheered me on!

I only seek powers to change the lots
Of our people, so blessed but live in penury
Ayuba knows I had good intentions
For us, my kinsmen
But our oppressors are as crafty as the crab,
Pulling down anyone who refuses to dance
The idiotic dance of slavery

Group: Ha! But Baba Clark warned you!
He cried to the rooftops and sang
The dirge of Orukorere* to warn you to beware
'Beware,' he warned you, our son

Solo: Yes, he warned me! But he too has his own fault

He sought the world, not for Ayuba's children,
But for himself, I dreaded his obscene calls for caution
They reeled my head like cannons that scared witches
Out of their covens
Indeed, as a people, we revel the song of grey heirs
But when it seeks gold in the altar of truth,
It is only fit for the pigs

Group: What about us? What did you do for us your kinsmen?
This is Otuoke, drained of its life
Before the eyes of its children
You brought us a university
But left us in darkness,
Groping dark with kerosene lamps
In the days when electricity lights up the world of others
Our roads are beautified by potholes
Mmm, Ayuba!
Indeed, your son has returned home, a hero!

Solo: If I failed the clan, you too must share in the blame
Oh yes! You too must share in the blame
The day I went to Abuja was the day you killed me
The Niger Delta belongs to us all,
Yet, you only speak the Izon tongue
To flay my vision

Our land suffers from series of ceaseless rapes,
The fangled creek of the delta is reddened with
The blood of our brave men
But you only cry in the Izon tongue
I left the other clans and piled up your greedy
Pockets with senseless gold
I bargained with strangers with our blood
Just to make you eat your inheritance in one swoop
'Your son is the president ye,

Herding South

Oil no dey finis ye!' you all cried
You only cried in the Izon tongue
Instead of the Niger Delta that gave us being
Whenever I raise my voice in the truce of *egbesu**
You cheered me on,
And we danced in Aso-Rock
Remembering only our leaking pockets
But the day the hawks came to enact
The fangled history of the land,
You all left me naked
Now, I am with you in Otuoke, without victory,
To eat farina and iced fish in the company
Of kerosene lamps while the oil companies
Light up their yards

Peter Omoko

The Emperor in the Ivory Tower

Hear, all
The emperor comes to town
Tiny grasses of the earth
Hide your daunting swag in shame
Who will stand eye-to-eye
With the emperor when men
Shiver in trepidation
As the herders herd south?

In the ivory tower of my harrowing land
The VC is the emperor of all
Other colleagues are subjects, seeking vents to survive
Their voices eaten up in their mouth – tongue quaking
Daring weaver birds' fate are sealed
As slothful professors grope about like zombies,
Waving painful hands in the sky
Each wetting his pants at the festival of query-letters,
Herding south

Today,
If we don't kill injustice in our Ivory Towers
We will all die piecemeal
Our disgraced necks hanging on the trees
To the victory of pompous injustice
For the day the university dies,
We all die,
Leaving the south to herdsmen!

The Flames of Our Blood

The hawks have again gathered
To enact the quadrupled rituals
Of dry bones impaled by dewdrops
Shaming partymen who wear mortal blood
Yet play the divine wand that stretched longer
Than freedom, pumping bullets into the loins
Of radical brats, caught in
The wanton spectacle of power

The diadem of our past haunts the feet of
Petulant priests who cook fables for sleepy initiates:
That hawks may smother beyond their deaths,
They peck on the flesh of frogs,
Serenaded in the blue gauge of the sea
Where they sacked our hearts in the pit of fantasies
Now, they have swallowed all that gave us hope,
Spat on the noxious sinews of our testis
And moulded us into baboons

But the sun will rise,
In the flames of our blood
That their mortal blood may dry out
Howling feverish flames that blind their eyes,
Hitting their heads against Aso-Rock

That day,
We shall rise,
Breaking the chains of hegemony,
Crafted on the breast of the land
With an assault known only to Major Walker
May the sea give us life,
May the forest give us shade,
May the mangrove give us strength
That we may dance to mock their mortal blood

The Cast Away

We all, weak
Bunch of tendril sap
Transfixed to regional ties
Without soul-searching mane
Soaked in talons of vultures

We are pawns
Young and simple
Easily exchanged
For the manipulations of
Knights, Bishops or maybe Queens

We the youths
Traversing the coronary of a nation
Blind and deadened by the
Skirmishes of mudskippers
Who party away many futures!

We, the singers of future tunes
Left in perpetual shipwreck
On a turbid and sticky streams,
Bemoaned only by owls
Bad omen of moonless nights
Though they refused us being,
Casting fragrance of fear within
We, the torch bearers of the future,
Are leading the way from behind!

The Bunkering Song

You smuggled her in torn pants,
And broken brassieres through the fangled creeks
Of Bemogbene* and Otor-Edo*
As darkness blinds the eyes of the sky.
River gods, dampened in their shrivelled clothes,
Are afraid of hegemonic poachers who elongate
Their greed to claim senile colony of ants
Coloured in crude and gas, torn apart

You smuggled her in torn pants,
Dragging her draped breasts through worthless offerings
As her raw cunt slaps the eyes of passersby in seductive darts
And you brag of taking a slice of your inheritance

Obogoma, why have you chosen to murder
The clan in the pot of oil bunkering;
In mounted greed,
To eat your inheritance in the dark!
You bunker and stalk the earth with death
In this marshy dung of hell,
Spread across dying forests,
Polluted streams,
Hissing mangroves,
And roasted sky!

Obogoma, your leaking kegs
Vomit death into the sinews of the land,
The burning pots of your greed clog the shoulders
Of our blood as the stench of roasted crudes
Clanks the roots of weeds and creepers in the niger delta
In this modular of doom, erected
To desecrate the clan

Truly, our oppressors promised us operating licenses
To own legitimate modular refineries
To cuddle the breasts of the crudes in our backyards
But were soon possessed by demons
The day fortune tellers danced on the Rock.
That horrible nightmare scared the gods
And mermaid left our shores

But,
When the head is broken,
The shoulder takes responsibility to wedge the blood
And so, Obogoma, you mounted on mountain tops
And smuggled naked crudes into the clan
To refine death in naira
That bribes nomadic policemen
Who collect toll of one thousand naira
      Per keg
           To
                  Keep watch
                      Of herders,
                            Herding south

The Day Papa Tip-toed into the Night

I have heard of the cooing of the dove,
The chirping of parrots' herd in
An evening flight across the sea
The wind had kissed the lips of forest trees
As they waved their heads in romantic fluff
The fog spreads its white garment in the bosom
Of the stream, calling the steerman of
The spirit boat
And then silence....

A murderous silence like the swag
Of white clothes across the face
Of corpses in a morgue

The iroko tree has shed the remains
Of its precious leaf,
The masquerade now danced naked,
The cock crowed in a tainted voice
Taunting the dewdrops of silence
Amid procession of weary hyacinths
Slugged to the shore by tired tides
Pale grasses sleep in the oily mud
That sticks to the throat of murderers
The clan wail; men and women,
Still and silent, folded their hands
Across their breasts in monologue,
Whimpering the communal dirge

That day,
The herders slept in their migration
To the south, the spirit market end, unannounced
The early morning tea, prepared by Aghogho*
Covered its face with the cyst of brown steam

Peter Omoko

Fearing the gaze of a lifeless body,
Steadied on an armchair of passage
Facing a smiling photograph of mama
Warped by the silent drum of death
Three years earlier as if to usher in
A new convert to the precinct of the ancestors

That night,
The dirge was hummed across the clan

Ghost Dance

The sheer gamut
Of kindred, in…
Fluctuation –
Of hawks – swinging in ecstasy
Of opposed parallel string,
Cutting through the brainy carapace
Of mutilated sorrows,
Souls die alone of thirst
Hands folded in king-fishing mourning
Suffer the muse of toxic regrets

Dreams unfulfilled…
Trouble the heart sore
Known moons in thick heaviness
Of deeds of decades, cry out!

At the confluence of foot paths
The crossroads where divinities sought
The sublime wishes of devotees
In white apparel of purity,
To placate the night with swollen entreaties
Full of daggers for the eyes at dawn
Marks and counts…
Disease of the mind, foot and will
Summons of unwillingness
Dying and resuscitating
This now and then
All in one fashion of tasteless routine
Dying and resuscitating
This now and then…
Across this marshy path
Where the tides skip!
Drowning the pregnant sea

Alas! They fed fat!
Always taking, never giving
Like the anopheles,
If it does give,
It spews lavae of rheumatism
…dreaded, to the death of all

Mourners

The river
      Mourns,
Bidding farewell
           To mocking
                Waves
Heaven in
      Piteous posture
                Winks
As raging storm
         Slaps and tosses
Sluggish
    Sea-weeds
          Along…

Our Crime

Fancies of personae
In growth and maturation of ideas
Of personal egos of fear and hope
In reverie of sanity.
Tumours,
           Aches,
                      Thought bulging:
We were all parked –
Like the herds of cattle,
Streamlining the southern savannah
To forage for jobs in centres
Where heads of ministries sat to fool all.

Though certain of their fooleries:...
In drowsy numbness we all cheer and cry
In piteous escapade of hopelessness.
Two or one of tens in budded strand,
Of job seekers walking in weeping motions –
Mothers with clasped children behind, jobless!
Young men with rich certificates, jobless!
Being tossed in opulent drains...
Day and night in their dreams.

... And here in billboard success;
Governors boast of delivering promises
To petty souls:
Jobs without pay,
Projects without contractors,
Programmes without beneficiaries
All in a ghostly three point agenda!

If I sit here seeking a job, their job,
My muse would desert me
And my ink dry up.

Cast a Spell

Among nursing mothers shrieking in fright
We journeyed.
As the brooding waves spread their jealous wings
Amidst the heaven's thundering voice
Each man to his God, called
To cast spell on innocent death.
Ayelala*, Tamara*, Osonobrughwe*, Ọlọrun*
Each man unto God, called.

And then the wild wind,
In a roaring expletive
Swept through the sea amidst angry waves
Tossing our old rickety boat to knock off bars
The propeller propels no more
And as indescribable wave builds in the heights.
Each man unto God, called
To cast spell on innocent death.
Ayelala, Tamara, Osonobrughwe, Ọlọrun
Each man unto God, called.

Each man to his ancestor called!
Olokun the sea goddess, cried her worshipers,
To win her grace.
     And
Send the sea to a sound sleep.
And each man to his star thank
As laughter was held on both sides.

Who Dem Help?

Dem come,
Sit down, with fat necks
Like hippopotamus
Dem bele sef e big
Like Mabel own for Central Hospital
For Warri
Wetin dem come tell us?
If no be our sense
Dem come collect again
With shinkini money

Help me ask dem,
Na who dem help?

From Iyara to Mc-Demot Road
Na dysentery dey kill small pikin
Edukugho na dungeon
Where rat dey shout for house-owner
Sake of say food no dey
For Igbudu and Akpologbe
Na weed dey keep
Our sanity for one place
Yet dem come tell us somtin'

Help me ask dem,
Na who dem help?

For Effurun Sapele Road
Bus no fit balance oga
Conductor don get sack letter
Keke don break okada leg
Go-slow don comot food

From *oga* bank manager mouth
Because dem carry Lagos road
Come put for Warri without plan
Yet dem say make we give
Dem our sense again

Help me ask dem,
Na who dem help?

Orhuwhorun na case study
Road safety, traffic police
And Nigerian army
Gather for road com hold meeting
'Your paper no correct'
Dem go shout
'Your side mirror don old'
Dem go talk
'Dat wan na bukable offence
You don enter wahala'
If you protest, you go frog-jump
Papa go late for work
Mama go late for shop
Pikin go late for skool
Taxi engine go cry-out for over-heat
Nobody get nobody time
Pregnant woman sef
Com born pikin for inside bus
And dem say make we listen to dem

Help me ask dem,
Na who dem help?

Glossary

Aghogho: the poet's younger sister

Akoro: a tree whose stem is used as chewing stick by the people of the Niger Delta

Amabolowei: A male deity in Ijaw.

Aso Rock: the seat of power and the official residence of Nigeria's President in Abuja

Ayelala: the Ilaje name for God.

Ayuba: the Izon name for God

Aziza: A half human/half spirit personality with one leg believed by the Urhobo to move with the wind.

Babalawos: Diviners

Bemogbene: one of the non-Ijaw camps in Odimodi, present day Burutu Local Government Council of Nigeria

Boko-Haram: an Islamic jihadist militant organisation based in north-eastern Nigeria

Egbada: Urhobo war dance-song

Egbesu: the Ijaw god of war and justice

Eshu: the Urhobo word for devil. Also used to express wickedness

Kweke: exclamation

Ifa: Divination

Mein: the ancestor of the western Ijaw people of the Niger Delta

Miyetti Allah: Cattle Breeders Association in the north

NEPA: National Electric Power Authority – responsible for the generation and distribution of electricity in Nigeria.

Oedipus: the Greek tragic hero of Sophocle's *King Oedipus*, fated to kill his father and marry his mother

Oloibiri: found in present-day Bayelsa State, this is reputed to be the place where oil was first discovered in commercial quantity in Nigeria in 1956.

Olokun: goddess of the sea and fortune.

Ọlọrun: the Yoruba name for God.

Orukorere: Zifa's half-possessed aunt in J.P. Clark's *Song of a Goat*. She is cursed by the sea gods of the land to see visions which no one believes because of her refusal to be their handmaiden.

Otor-Edo: an Ughievwen village in present-day Ughelli South Local Government Council of Nigeria noted for clay deposit

Osonobrughwe: the Urhobo name for God.

Tamara: another Ijaw name for God.

Tẹbẹsọnọma of the Seven Heads: one of the warriors defeated by Ozidi junior in J.P. Clark's *The Ozidi Saga*

Udje: one of the classical song-poetry traditions of the Urhobo people

www.ingramcontent.com/pod-product-compliance
Lightning Source LLC
Chambersburg PA
CBHW011957150426
43200CB00018B/2935